Poetry With Family

JOSEPH PREMAL JAYAKUMAR

AuthorHouse™ UK Ltd.
1663 Liberty Drive
Bloomington, IN 47403 USA
www.authorhouse.co.uk
Phone: 0800.197.4150

Published by AuthorHouse

ISBN: 978-1-4918-7936-8 (sc)

Rev. Date: 09/19/2013

Any people depicted in stock imagery provided by Thinkstock are models,
and such images are being used for illustrative purposes only.
Certain stock imagery © Thinkstock.

This book is printed on acid-free paper.

authorHOUSE®

Poetry With Family

JOSEPH PREMAL JAYAKUMAR

Table Of Contents

Very Very Sorry

I gave a word

That I never kept

I gave a desire

That I never shared

I gave hope

That I never bestowed

I gave light

That I never shed

I gave strength

That I never proved

I gave life

That I never lived

I gave trust

For that I am very very sorry

A bye never said

I will fly

To the sky

As you imply,

With a sigh.

Never you cry,

For a bye

You never reply.

Always remain high.

However I try,

Always you deny.

Will only obey,

Your every lie.

Will never annoy

Till I die.

Be at joy

My Helene of Troy.

Mother's Best

I am the best

Any man can get

I am the best

Any father can wish for

I am the best

Any friend can hold onto

I am the best

A wife can trust upon

I am the best

A son can ever dream of

I am the best

Any girl can be with

I am the best

A brother can yearn

I am the best

The nature has ever made

I am the best

Any woman can desire

I am the best

In character anyone possess

I am the best

Any child can play with

I am the best

To the one in dire need

I am the best

Any team can comprise

I am the best

A human to show compassion

I am the best

A king in giving

I am my mother's best . . . .

Walking Back

Wish to walk back

The lanes of childhood again

Where no worries to stack

And a heart without pain.

Nobody to stare,

How carefree a life

Full of fanfare

And innocence beyond belief.

Everyone seems a pal then

And every moment is for play.

Always laughing though in heaven,

A real paradise to stay.

Being naughty always

With nothing to hide.

Yearn to live those days

Once again as my mother's child.

A Bahraini Lady

The best way to wear a hijab

Should be learnt from a Bahraini lady.

The best way to smile

Should be seen from a Bahraini lady.

The best way to live

Should be copied from a Bahraini lady.

The best way to be bold

Should be imbibed from a Bahraini lady.

The best way to be beautiful

Should be asked from a Bahraini lady.

The best way to be fearless

Should be imitated from a Bahraini lady.

The best way to be kind

Should be inherited from a Bahraini lady.

The best way to ethically work

Should be inspired from a Bahraini lady.

The best way to be courteous

Should be embraced from a Bahraini lady.

Finally the best way to be called "bhaiya"

Should be heard from a Bahraini lady.

I am done

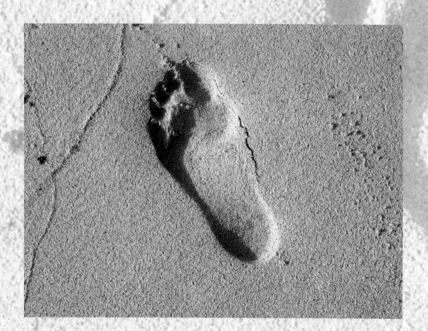

I run

In all hearts

But stay in none

Because of my acts.

Wish at least someone

See the facts,

Before they shun

And break me to parts.

I am full of fun

And best in arts

But that doesn't stun,

Nor add me to anyone's charts.

I am done

In this world of rots.

Lead me to light

You have crossed high seas,

Covered vast miles,

Mustered so much might,

From every plight.

Yet so humble in grace.

I am just a kid on knees,

Can never reach your scales.

Show me some light

From this darkness, holding me tight,

By sharing your best of phrase.

A life worth living

Give me a *sight*

I shall *write* you a sonnet

Give me a *smile*

I shall walk a *mile* with you

Give me a *look*

I shall *hook* to your every moment

Give me a *space*

I shall *embrace* you forever

Give me a *hug*

I shall *bug* you all day

Give me a *motive*

I shall *live* the rest for you

Give me a *sigh*

I shall *cry* a lifetime for you

Give me a *wish*

I shall *vanish* with your memories cherished

Give me a *word*

I shall *trod* the world with that

Give me a *chance*

I shall *romance* your entire life

Give me a *second*

I shall *pleasant* you immense

Give me an *hour*

I shall *never* stop describing you ever

Give me a *day*

I shall *stay* awake gazing you

Give me a *still*

I shall *fulfil* your every dream

Give me your *heart*

I shall *start* a new beginning

Give me a *life*

I shall *wife* you eternally hereafter

Give me a *dish*

I shall *finish* leaving half for you

Give me a *hope*

I shall *stop* myself from being old

Give me an *offspring*

I shall *bring* back our beauty to relive

Give me a *kiss*

I shall *miss* you never in this lifetime

Give me your *hand* for the last time

I shall *land* in HIS arms anytime soon

Give me an *end*

I shall not *repent* any life thereafter . . .

Give me a whisper

Lost the flare

As silence can tear,

And ruin many a pillar,

However strong from inner.

Give me a second to spare

And show me that you care.

At least a weak whisper,

My beautiful flower.

I ask only to share,

Since this pain, difficult to bear.

Tell me my mother,

Should I dream her ever?

Ego is my middle name.

Sorry if I may hurt

As am covered by this ego dirt.

Still you will love to impart

My persona, which is my highest fort.

Hence ask you to be in my cart.

Bear me, I tell, before we start.

Will not curse, if you now depart.

Will only count as another painful dart.

I try to change some sort

But that will not be my true part.

Though I was never a great to be that smart

You shall still miss this witty brat at heart.

Everything good stands out

A good line

Can taste better than old wine

A good note

Can be heard from a mother's throat

A good beat

Can help forget defeat

A good tune

Can improve the immune

A good compose

Can be wonder as the frescoes

A good voice

Can bring closer to paradise

A good dance

Can put anyone to a trance

A good artiste

Can make any twist

A good audience

Can applaud in elegance.

When can I be myself?

When can I fly

As a bird

Without a worry of abode?

When can I sleep

In the open

Watching the horizon?

When can I fight justice

Like before

Without holding back no more?

When can I write a poem

In peace

With only my memories?

When can I play

Like at school

High in spirit only to rule?

When can I work

Without fear

Of being insecure?

When can I live

In pious

A life of my choice?

When can I laugh

With innocence

Never showing any hindrance?

When can I express love

To anyone dear

Without any form of fear?

When can I help the poor

In need

Without any calls to heed?

When can I see the world

In my own eyes

Without any advice.

My Silent Beauty

Through the eyes of doe,

Her emotions flow.

By the rhythmic walk,

Her sound body talk.

With the grace of silence,

Her sweet words commence.

In the leafy eyebrows,

Her womanly aura grows.

Using the caring heart,

Her feelings rise to comfort.

Having the luminous smile,

Her presence is worthwhile.

Farewell

May you get the prince you desire

And together you reign glory.

In that land of happiness,

I shall live as your obedient subject.

May you tower even higher

With hundred little ones to empty your every worry.

In that heaven of oneness,

I shall see the beauty of life you reflect.

Mother Nature

How beautiful is nature

Whose beauty we all envy,

With its sun, moon and all living creature,

So amazing which makes us merry

The fabulous oceans that never rest,

With its enchanting waves,

Kissing one another at its best,

Find time to admire nature's plays.

ALL ALONE

My ever long companion is loneliness.

From my childhood to adulthood,

This friendship between us never became any less.

I always try to be good,

To win at least a single heart.

In vain goes my try

As everyone tear be apart.

I almost give a cry

But my inner spirit forbids

And says you are not all alone.

These are all nature's wits,

Be with her and your worries will be flown.

A TRUE GIFT OF NATURE

Trees and plants are the greatest jewel in nature's crown,

With these she shows off her admirable beauty.

The fabulous coloured flowers replace every king's throne,

In their presence we feel our worries empty.

The greenery surrounding the Earth makes it a paradise.

We should be blessed to receive such a valuable gift.

To admire and love it requires a big heart to sacrifice.

After all without them we would have never remained fit.

HAPPINESS

It comes to us like a blessing

When our minds are filled with joy

Keeping us always smiling

Making the day a time of glory.

It departs us like a lightning

When our minds are filled with fury

Sending us reeling

Making the day a time of worry.

MOTHER-A DIVINE CREATION

O mother, you are the universe.

From you, evolves every life.

All resources persist in you.

All my riches are your blessing.

When in despair, you chant the verse

That drizzles out my entire grief

Making me like a glistening dew

We see in the dawn during the birds sing.

Your love to me is sweet

As the nectar of the Lord.

Your care for me is bright

As the halo of the Sun.

I bow and touch your feet

To forgive my every harsh word,

Since the age of mine is like a kite,

Sometimes violent and sometimes fun.

MY LOVELY GIRL

My girl is full of love and care

And her heart is full of me.

She is very precious and rare

Like the pearls found in the sea.

Every moment with her I treasure

And every smile of her I adore.

Her beauty is beyond measure

And I love her from the core.

UTTER DESPERATION

When everything comes to a standstill,

When everything drifts from the clutches,

When everyone turns with indifference,

When the mind gets drenched in sadness,

When the unexpected happens,

When the loved ones leave halfway,

When losing the battle is the only option,

The heart aches against our will,

The spirits and morale fall into the ditches,

The strong calibre loses its cadence,

The everlasting smile loses its fairness,

The iron instincts loses its stance,

Any strong man feels moved and at bay,

A condition of utter desperation.

The True Beauty

Be open minded and fair,

It makes you glare.

Remove jealous and hatred,

It makes you sacred.

Love everybody wholly.

It makes you holy.

Expect nothing in return,

It makes you govern.

Never turn away anyone,

It makes you as God's son.

Help everyone to your best,

It makes you always first.

Always keep your word,

It makes you leap forward.

Never utter anything brute,

It makes you everybody's fruit.

Be committed to your duty,

These all give you the true beauty.

My Dream Girl

She comes to me when the Sun goes down

From a peaceful village, in a beautiful skirt and blouse

And stays close to me calling me a clown,

Talking to me to console me of my day's sorrows.

Her presence gives me the greatest relief

As I have no one to love me sincerely.

She gives away a smile that solves my every grief,

She scolds me like a child for being all day lonely.

If without her I would be perished,

As she is my every satisfaction.

She leaves me with a lot of memories cherished

Though this is only a good imagination.

A Mother's Milk

The pure waters pour from above,

Making millions of bubbles below,

So nice to watch they float

Like the thousand ships, once set to plot.

She fills every place with joy

Like how the stars fill the sky.

She smiles with her rainbow,

Telling us she is a friend and not a foe.

Everyone welcomes her arrival

With great pomp and marvel,

From the smallest of seed

To the entire living breed.

She is full of beauty,

Like a lady in sari.

She is a sacred omen,

A mother's milk to every Human.

The Final Journey

All is gone

What remains is in a pot full.

Even the air

Is not there anymore to take.

All that left

Is mere memories of deeds done.

How you lived

Is what materially eternally.

What you did

Nice to your fellow beings counts.

At least a few generations

Should know your service.

Hence there might

Be someone to take you in the final journey.

You can but cannot

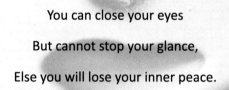

You can hold you mind

But cannot forget my thoughts,

As it will always follow you behind.

You can close your eyes

But cannot stop your glance,

Else you will lose your inner peace.

You can refuse to speak

But cannot stop listening to my words,

Be it however bleak.

You can hold your heart

But cannot stop the beat of love it sounds,

However you be smart.

You can avoid my sight

But cannot stop your instincts

From seeing me with much delight.

Love -A Sacred Phenomenon

True love emanates from one's heart.

It is a mutual devotion towards one another.

In the midst of this, every other attachment fades away.

Loving hearts can never stay apart.

However one hides, it blooms like a flower.

The loving emotions are as innocent as a child's play.

What causes such beautiful events is a mystery.

Love can never be sinful

Nor it can disdain any living soul.

The only requirement is to have a dignified character

And a glorious and sacred mind.

The journey of love is thorny as well as blissful.

Forgive, forget and fulfil each other should be the goal.

If one lacks these factors, he is only a mere actor.

The success of this cascade of compassion is to be always kind.

33

Love is like a flower

It evolves like

The blossoming of a flower,

It tastes like

Her nectar,

It shines like

The dew on her petals,

It blooms like

Her sweet scent,

It departs like

The way she falls.

Live naturally

Glow like the Sun,

Shine like the moon,

Twinkle like the stars,

Shower like the rain,

Flow like a breeze,

Whistle like a wind,

Vanish like a ripple,

Leave with a thunder.

Not even once . . . .

Not even once did you enquire

About my good health,

Not even once did you bid

Me good bye,

Not even once did you wish

Me good times,

Not even once did you ask

Me how I was,

Not even once did you obey

My simple requests,

Not even once did you make

Me a happier person,

Not even once did you pamper

Me as a child,

Not even once did you sacrifice

A second from your life for me,

Not even once did you come

To me passionately,

Not even once did you say

A nice word to my ears,

Not even once did you write back

For my thousand words,

Not even once did you give

Me a place to stay in your heart..

Please open up . . .

I can know you, only if you throw me

With words in plenty.

I can see you, only if you carry me

In your heart without fear of any.

I can love you, only if you allow me

To be that person lucky . . . .

A request never asked

Can you give me a hand

To raise me to command,

Can you spare me a thought

To water my drought,

Can you pass me a smile

To keep me agile,

Can you give me a line

To lift me from decline,

Can you be with me always

To bring back my witty old days?

Watch out

Sometimes a small stone shall sink

A ship that survived such a stormy sea,

Which safely sailed, soldiering such a sever shrink,

Only to be shaken by a simple rock so silly.

FAMILY

F-Feeling of oneness arise within this sphere,

A-Affection grows without any fear,

M-Maturity is attained from here,

I-Intimacy among members is instinctively clear,

L-Love is seen in its every layer,

Y-Yearn to be a part of this forever.

Be happy to worry

I see no terrain

Full of joy and free from pain.

Those reaching heaven may claim to gain,

Yet to reach there you have to be sans air, lying plain.

So enjoy both like lightning and rain,

If one scares so loud other helps life to sustain,

Always inseparable and together in twain,

Like husband and wife, united but mostly complain.

Hence both are needed to keep us in the right lane,

Else it's not life, where only one shall remain.

A paradise to retreat

Tired of this running feat

In the name of making life, sweet,

Without even living a minute complete.

Never even finding time to nicely eat,

Where even siblings never get to nicely meet,

And never to one another extend a simple greet

Oh . . . . give me a paradise to retreat

To live at least for a single day in my own beat.

Have Hope

It's hope that keeps me still driving to you.

However hard you hold your view,

I believe that one day I can break this shell into few.

If not here then somewhere we shall start a life so new.

Against all odds I shall still pursue.

If not now then surely later you will join me too.

If not in this birth, I shall wait the next without a clue,

By sailing, hoping against hope into the blue.

If not today then someday I will lead you through,

If I don't win, until my memory fade, I shall live only to woo.

We live to die

The day has come to a close,

The night is waiting for my doze

And I am still alive to live another day,

Only to find when will be my final stay.

That's Earthly beauty, as we live to die,

May be to rise again as the stars of the sky.

Some stay long while some leave early,

Every being completing their natural line of duty.

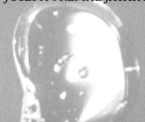

Never underestimate . . .

Don't push me to quit

As I may stand my ground never to budge a bit.

Don't try me to lose

As I may never give you that pose.

Don't put me to love

As I may conquer the best heart somehow

Don't press me to fall

As I may never make that call.

Don't treat me with ego

As I may never to it bow . . . .

Don't play me weak

As I may take the highest peak.

Don't take me light

As I may show the best of fight.

Don't go with me to battle

As I may win the bravest title.

Dearest mother..

I don't need to be a king

But only as a son under your wing.

If you are behind me

I shall cross any sea.

The love from you I cannot hold,

Will try to feel with my hands fold.

Please take me wherever you go

Else I shall never glow.

I bow to you my dearest mother,

As to be with you is truly an honour.

Printed in the United States
By Bookmasters